Karts

BY JACK DAVID

TORQUE

BELLWETHER MEDIA • MINNEAPOLIS, MN

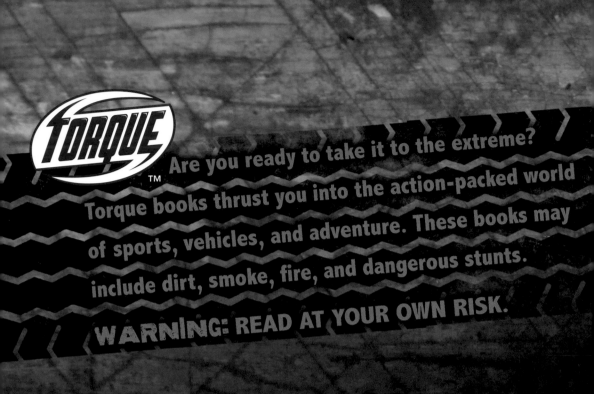

Are you ready to take it to the extreme?

Torque books thrust you into the action-packed world of sports, vehicles, and adventure. These books may include dirt, smoke, fire, and dangerous stunts.

WARNING: READ AT YOUR OWN RISK.

This edition first published in 2008 by Bellwether Media.

No part of this publication may be reproduced in whole or in part without written permission of the publisher. For information regarding permission, write to Bellwether Media Inc., Attention: Permissions Department, Post Office Box 19349, Minneapolis, MN 55419.

Library of Congress Cataloging-in-Publication Data

David, Jack, 1968-
  Karts / by Jack David.
      p. cm. -- (Torque--cool rides)
  Summary: "Amazing photography accompanies engaging information about Karts. The combination of high-interest subject matter and light text is intended for students in grades 3 through 7"--Provided by publisher.
  Includes bibliographical references and index.
  ISBN-13: 978-1-60014-149-2 (hardcover : alk. paper)
  ISBN-10: 1-60014-149-8 (hardcover : alk. paper)
  1. Cyclecars--Juvenile literature. 2. Karting--Juvenile literature. I. Title.

  TL390.D38 2008
  629.228--dc22
                                                                    2007040563

Contents

What Is a Kart?

Karts, also called go-karts, are lightweight race cars with an open-wheel design. This means the wheels sit outside the car's main body.

Karts are inexpensive and easy to handle. These features make kart racing among the most popular motor sports in the world for both kids and adults.

Fast FaCt

Kart drivers sit only about an inch above the ground.

Kart History

Art Ingels and Lou Borelli built the first kart in 1956. Ingels was a mechanic and a race car builder. He attached wheels, a seat, and a lawnmower motor to a steel frame. It was fast and fun to drive. Many people enjoyed his invention and copied the design.

Soon people began racing their karts. Some people just sped around empty parking lots. Others built special courses for races. The Go-Kart Club of America was formed in 1957. This organization helped set up rules for the growing sport.

Fast Fact
Karts with 250cc engines can
reach speeds of 140 miles
(225 kilometers) per hour!

Parts Of a Kart

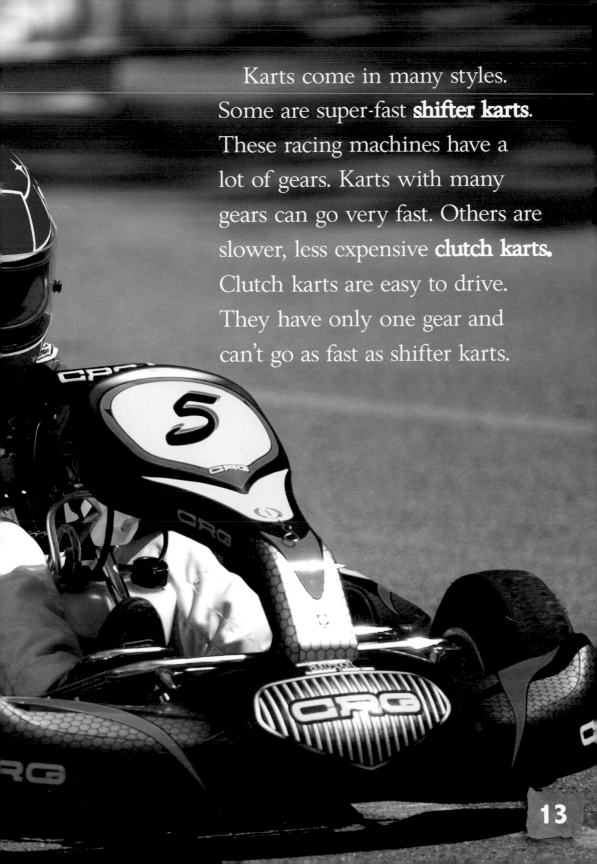

Karts come in many styles. Some are super-fast **shifter karts**. These racing machines have a lot of gears. Karts with many gears can go very fast. Others are slower, less expensive **clutch karts.** Clutch karts are easy to drive. They have only one gear and can't go as fast as shifter karts.

All karts share some common features. They start with a metal frame called a **chassis**. Most karts have lightweight body panels that fit over the chassis.

vodafone
Fast FaCt
Many famous drivers get their start in karts. Stock car stars Jeff Gordon and Tony Stewart drove karts. So did Indy Car champion Sam Hornish, Jr.

The **suspension system** and tires are important to a kart. The suspension system includes springs and shock absorbers. It connects the wheels to the chassis and gives a kart a smooth ride. Small, smooth tires called **slicks** give a kart a good grip on paved surfaces.

The engine sits behind the driver. Engine size is measured in cubic centimeters (cc). Karts for children, called kid karts, have engines as small as 50cc. Other karts have 250cc engines or larger. A large engine produces more power than a small one.

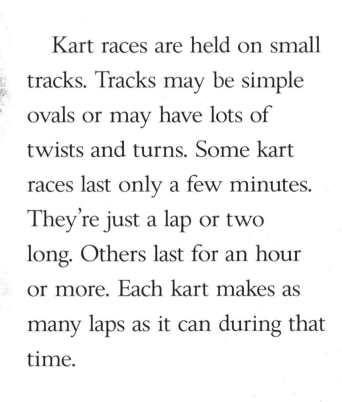

Karts in Action

Kart races are held on small tracks. Tracks may be simple ovals or may have lots of twists and turns. Some kart races last only a few minutes. They're just a lap or two long. Others last for an hour or more. Each kart makes as many laps as it can during that time.

Kart races have a fast pace and lots of action. Each race includes about 16 karts. They line up side by side, in two rows. Drivers take off when the green flag waves. They steer hard into each turn. They try to pass each other without crashing or spinning out. Only one driver can take the **checkered flag** and the victory.

Fast FaCt

Spinning out can be dangerous. Hay bales and tires are often put around tracks to safely stop drivers who lose control of their karts.

Glossary

chassis—the metal frame of a kart

checkered flag—the flag waved at the end of a race; the winner is said to "take the checkered flag."

clutch kart—a kart with a single gear

shifter kart—a kart with many gears

slicks—smooth racing tires

suspension system—the system of springs and shock absorbers that connects a kart's frame to its wheels

To Learn more

AT THE LIBRARY

David, Jack. *Go-Kart Racing*. Minneapolis, Minn.:
Bellwether, 2008.

Doeden, Matt. *Shifter Karts*. Mankato, Minn.:
Capstone, 2005.

Herran, Joe, and Ron Thomas. *Karting*. Philadelphia,
Pa.: Chelsea House, 2004.

ON THE WEB

Learning more about karts
is as easy as 1, 2, 3.

1. Go to www.factsurfer.com

2. Enter "karts" into search box.

3. Click the "Surf" button and you will
   see a list of related web sites.

With factsurfer.com, finding more information is
just a click away.

Index

The images in this book are reproduced through the courtesy of: Joe Fox Motorsport/Alamy, front cover; jaggart, pp. 5, 6; Iain Farley/Alamy, p. 7; Sherman/Stringer/Getty Images, p. 9; LensCapp/Alamy, p. 10; Chris Young/Stringer/Getty Images, p. 11; Dyana/Alamy, pp. 12-13; Paul Gilham/Getty Images, pp. 14-15; Joe Fox/Alamy, pp. 16, 20-21; Frances Roberts/Alamy, p. 17; Carl Lyttle/Getty Images, p. 18.